The WHY Generation

In a Why Not World

The WHY Generation

In a Why Not World

MICHAEL J. CARNEY

ACTION PUBLISHING
WILMINGTON, DELAWARE

First edition: December 2021

10 9 8 7 6 5 4 3 2 1

TABLE OF CONTENTS

THE ESSAYS

THE POEMS

This book is dedicated to three great Americans that I respect, love and cherish. They are Thomas Jefferson, Samuel "Mark Twain" Clemens, and Edward Fordham, my grandfather.

FOREWORD

It is 1976. Thirteen years have passed since J.F.K. was killed. We are still not sure who was responsible for his death. The latest theory is that Castro, the Cuban dictator, ordered his agents to kill Kennedy in retaliation for similar attempts on his life by the CIA. Two Mafia type characters were recently found murdered who were allegedly recruited by the CIA to kill Castro. Lee Harvey Oswald and Jack Ruby had mysterious connections with Cuba. It is still a mystery.

As I look out at this beautiful fall day, I think about the many events that have shaped our lives in the last thirteen years. I sit in the college library and watch the faces of today's young students. They seem to lack the rebellious intensity that I experienced during the '60s here on campus. I hear them speak about jobs and getting married. They are not trying to change the world, screw the system or end the war, as my fellow students were in my college days. What has happened during the last thirteen years is the subject of this book.

People, places and events are historical record. Yet the thoughts, moods, feelings, and true aspirations are my main concern.

I believe that for the first time in the history of man a why generation has developed. It is not limited by age, race, sex or national origin. It is not just youth rebelling against tradition, which has happened since the beginning of time. It is a meaningful search and discussion of the values, motives and needs of mankind. People who belong to this why generation will not stop asking the questions "why" to questionable practices until they find better answers. The old standby reply from authority to youth that "You are too young to understand" or "That's the way the world turns" is a lame, rejected argument.

In high school, I had an English teacher who taught us that it was the responsibility of each new generation to question the values and morale of the preceding generation. They must choose to accept or reject them as society constantly evolves. Well, this generation has done more than accept or reject—they have established a philosophy and a way of life that constantly challenges and attempts to correct the existing order. It is more than just not taking no for an answer. It is a dedicated, honest search for the answer to the questions "why?" Why must I go to church every week? Why are there unjust wars? Why do we have ghettos? Why do I not have control over my own body? Why must I accept lower pay for equal work to other races or sexes? Why must I eat, drink or breathe poison? Why must I work for another power? We also ask greater questions. Why do I exist? Why do I not love my neighbor? Why does God allow unhappiness? Why must I believe in God? Why is there a government? Why can't I get answers? This list goes on almost forever. The answers are sometimes simple but usually difficult to find or understand, but the true searchers of the why generation believe that there are answers if we're willing to pay the price to find them.

This book will tell the story of paying the price for these answers. Through a collection of poems, essays and pictures, I will show the important value discoveries of the why generation.

We reject the "why not if you can get away with it" morality. There has got to be a better way. Hail the coming of the new day. O hail the why generation in a why not world.

The WHY Generation

In a Why Not World

LIFE, I LOVE YOU

Life, I love you, always changing
Never doubting or asking for more.
How should I walk in your beauty?
For unlike nature I meet my match.

1.

CHESS AND LIFE

For the people who do not understand the movements and respective powers of each chess piece, I ask your indulgence. You will be able to see and understand the comparison between chess and life without a thorough education in either.

There are too many people in this world to waste your time with, so you should pick a few close friends, be loyal to them, and enjoy their friendship. Picking friends sometimes involves declaring enemies. I do not want to paint the world in black and white. It is logical that if you do not take someone on your side that wants to be there, he or she may feel resentment and join other sides, often against you. The chess board is designed for opposing pieces to move, attack and conquer the opponent's pieces. There are pawns who are limited people with little influence. There are religious leaders called Bishops who sit by the King and Queen for advice and protection. They can also destroy in a long, sweeping, diagonal attack. There are castles and fortresses that protect the royalty from both sides. There are knights that can jump over others in their enthusiasm to capture. They are sometimes the greatest fighters in the game. Of course, there is a Queen that has all the combined powers of the lower order. Ironically, the King and most important prize in the game, has the least ability to defend or attack. He must use others to advance his causes. If this somewhat colorful description seems like a few friends or enemies of yours, such as the government, C.I.A., the local minister, priest, or rabbi, or maybe your employer, fellow employees, or perhaps your neighbors and relatives, it has been a successful analogy. In everyone's life, there are people who do not feel they are important. They are some times poor, uneducated or just unloved. Most of all they are powerless. In this "survival of the fittest" world, they live unhappy lives—they are pawns. We are prejudiced against them. We deny them success. We forbid them love and throw them a bone now and then to keep them under control. These minorities often attack other minorities not realizing that if they united together they could reach great goals and greater power.

People who defend you and help you get places are your strongest friends. Choose these knights well. Teach them when to attack and retreat because they can remove great obstacles to your success in life. Good friends are rare so always be loyal to them. The reward you will receive will be equal to the amount of support and affection you give to your inner circle of admirers.

The Bishops of life have much to say, usually too much. They may be in-laws, managers, parents, or religious authorities. The often think they know more than you. Accept their advice with respect, but choose your own path, follow your own star, or you be left trapped in a corner of nothingness. People who live entirely for other people have not lived at all.

In every family there should be a King and Queen. They live in the same castle, watch the same show and participate in the same game. For the greatest happiness, they must cooperate. When they argue, they are left unguarded. If one leaves the other is much weaker. The conflict between these two can destroy the game of life for both. The smart player keeps his strength together and employs them separately only when it is for the good of both parties. Family unity makes a strong castle. It can be a true fortress against the attacks of a non-caring world. Remember your priorities and never be exactly the same as the next King or Queen. So work your own plans, live your own life. Shakespeare said, "Life is a comedy to those who think and a tragedy to those who feel." Think before you act. Let your reason overcome your emotion. May you love your friends, and may your checkmates always be few.

QUESTIONS LEFT UNANSWERED

All sides are done shouting,
The nasty noises have now been silenced
Yet the puzzle still persists in the minds of the many
Whose questions are left unanswered.

Backlash, whiplash, Patton and MASH
All make one think it was a stalemated bash
Daddy doesn't know who won the war,
But he sure knows the answer to "What's the score?"

Involvement retracted, commitment neglected
The retreating followers have all defected.
This eye in the storm has a paradoxical form
That leads me to fear that the why generation has
reverted to beer.

2.

WORK

Work has become synonymous with drudgery, unhappiness and forced labor. It is sad that in today's supposedly enlightened age, we take such a dim view of an important part of our lives. Statistics from surveys indicate that the majority of people hate their work. It is ironic that the same pollsters do not ask the individual if he despises his clothes, his car, his house, T.V. or any other symbol of his life style. The worker seems to forget the fruits of his labor. To put work in its proper perspective, you should define it. When you work for a business or government, you have voluntarily decided to sell your talents, time and services to this buyer for an agreed upon price. The price is your wage or salary that you have agreed to in good faith. The reason this wage for your work may not be high in your opinion is because your talents are not worth much, or you have sold yourself too cheaply. Most people blame their bosses for their situation, yet it is the employee who has a low opinion of himself. If you want to attain riches for your time and services, you should develop highly sellable talents. This is common sense, and anyone can do it. No one is truly enslaved in the free world capitalist system. If you want more, make yourself worth work more. Horatio Alger felt that "luck, pluck and decency" are the most important elements in achieving success in America. He was close to the truth, but too many disgruntled workers laugh at his ideas. When you consider that it does take some luck to be in the right place at the right time, meaning having the right talents that can be sold to the most lucrative buyers, he is correct. Pluck meaning trying your best, or having persistence, and positive attitudes. There are some that cut corners and cheat their employers, yet seem to get promotions. Their riches are short lived. You would much rather work with someone who knew what he was doing and believed in his ability to get the job done rather than a work shirker, wouldn't you? You do not need a phony image to achieve status or success. A decent person tries not to let his personal problems affect his bargain with the employer. It may be hard to do but you do not want to hear about your boss's sick wife and broken transmission when you pick up your paycheck, do you? Why should he sacrifice his efficiency for your outside influences? People who are unemployed think very little of their talents or have no true desire to develop them. They are too proud to take a menial job when that is all they are really worth, yet have no pride at all about taking the honest hardworking man's tax dollar to support their laziness. I realize this seems a hard line with little sympathy, but it is only a small minority who can work and will not. These parasites deserve the life style they own.

Individuals who own companies are tremendous leaders, no matter how great or trivial their product or service they produce, they are an essential ingredient in our work system. A man or woman who hires you should earn your mutual respect because he wants to share his idea with you. He has invested a lot of money and time in a product or service and has offered you the choice of joining him in his endeavor. Whether you share his enthusiasm or not, you should honor your contract by using your talents to serve the common purpose. We think too often that only a few people enjoy their work and do anything worthwhile with their lives. This is immature reasoning because anyone can enjoy the hours they are being paid by honestly doing their can best. This wins the respect of their friends and neighbors by producing a good product or delivering a needed service. The street cleaner who keeps the city's streets free from health or dangerous filth and unsightly litter can be and usually is happier than the overpaid professional who overcharges his clients.

THE AMERICAN FLAG IN THE MORNING

I am sure that Key said it better than me,
But I feel that I must agree.
The bright stars and broad stripes that now I see
Have flown proudly throughout our history.

The flag in the morning is a dazzling sight
As the breeze extends it from left to right
Let liberty fly and all see its light
I am reminded again of the historical fight.

The blood that was spilled was bright American red
The color of the skin was white, yet dead.
The sky that left us was blue overhead
America the beautiful is what they all said.

Is the fight really over?
Has freedom been won?
Will the Dodgers be able to score another run?
The Americans work hard at their fun
There will always be tyranny under the sun.

As long as the mind is a slave to another
As sure as there are fights between brother and brother
George Washington is still our founding father
The world looks for hope to our American mother.

Liberty and opportunity are surely America's bag
The rights that are written are rarely allowed to sag
The Constitution we uphold is more than just a rag
All stand and salute the great American flag.

3.

SPORTS

After watching six hours of profession football on television, I feel I should explore the reasons for this visual gluttony. I played football with eleven friends for two hours Saturday morning and watched my college alma mater win 63 to 0 for three hours Saturday afternoon. I sometimes wonder whether I have become a slave to the sports syndrome in America. Since we do not have royalty or recent military heroes, it has become common to adore our sports figures. We cheer them one week and boo them the next one, expecting consistent winning battles all the time. They subject themselves to serious injury while they entertain the masses. It is important to note that they are paid exorbitant amounts of money to perform this service. The best professional athletes earn more than our national leaders and presidents of middle-sized corporations. I do not begrudge them their pay when they play their best. Many fans say that no man is worth $1 million or $6 million when it can easily be shown how increased attendance multiplied by ticket prices more than justify the huge contracts for superstars.

In 1926, the Olympic Games made Americans feel that they are something of a master race. Our gold medal winners stand to reap great fortunes from sponsors who want to identify with winners. Selling a product becomes much easier when you have a spokesperson who previously has proven himself in the thrill of international competition. Our decathlon winner, Bruce Jenner, sometimes acclaimed "the greatest athlete in the world," must be careful to whom he lends his endorsement. Our Olympic basketball team regained its prominence by winning the gold medal. We have won it in every Olympics except 1972, when we felt the referees cheated us and gave the game to the Russians. We were not given the pleasure of a rematch because their team did not make it to the finals in 1976. The point of all this common knowledge is to show how the individual can join emotionally with the team or national cause. When his team or country wins, he feels that he is part of that success. He thinks he has defeated the Russians, Japanese and Germans through his American Olympic team. When his favorite loses, he searches for excuses to explain why he was cheated of his glory. When a favorite team falters, we often divorce ourselves from them. We are never responsible for the defeats of our favorite sports heroes.

The amount of time and money spent on sports in this country is devastating. Gambling has become such a large part of our national pastime that it is not only unimportant who wins or loses or how you play the game; but it is essential only to beat the spread. This handicapping can make temporary heroes out of terrible athletes if they reward their financial supporters with a close game. I have yet to meet a person who gambles often and is a winner in real life. His family and business situations are usually in turmoil. He cannot hit home runs with people around him, so he bets on others. He can accuse and acclaim as though he owns every sports franchise that he wagers on so foolishly.

Violence in sports seems to be a favorite topic of journalists. Should boxing be banned? Is hockey only successful when fights occur at the game? Do blitzing linebackers, aggressive basketball centers, and spikes-flying base stealers all eat raw meat for breakfast? Why is there such violence in our growing sports tradition? The fans demand it. They feel pleasure in seeing the enemy experience pain. They enjoy the advantages of excessive physical efforts yet they are the first to scream when their heroes are destroyed by "cheap shots." I think the real cheap shot is the lack of concern we sports fans give the people around us that we love. I leave a warm bed and a loving wife at 8:30 on a Saturday morning to throw a pigskin around with 10 other "nuts" my age. It is fine to support your college football team but it is sick to cheer your team to kill an overmatched opponent when the score is 63 to 0. It is very wrong to miss church and say no to your wife when she asks you to do a favor during the pro football T.V. period from 1 p.m. to 7 on Sunday. It is inhuman to scream at her when you lose a bet because the team you didn't like anyway lost by 15 instead of 10 points. Sports can be dangerous to your emotional well being, and especially to people around you.

In conclusion, we sports fans must be our interest in the proper perspective. We must leave the game on the field and forget about it. Most importantly we must repeat to ourselves over and over, "It's only a game. It's only a game." Especially when our team loses.

MIDNIGHT REVELATION

A shining sky solved my problem
I was placed at ease by a flickering star
The cool air slowed my hurried pace
and asked me to stop and take a glance
at something that was more than me.

Yet my ego challenged the eternal light
I tried to reach up and kiss the night.
I missed my shot by a waste of time.
The night laughed and it hurt my pride.

I threatened to close it out of sight
It continued to haunt me, but I could not hide
I vowed revenge, but could do it no harm,
The system then grabbed me and I forgot that
I kissed the night and died at daybreak.

4.

LEISURE

I once had a philosophy professor who suggested that man's natural state of being was at play. We all laughed at this suggestion, realizing that our futures were filled with responsibilities of work and family. After all, didn't we go to college to learn a career and make our mark in the world. I can easily accept this philosophy when I think of the second childhood atmosphere of my college days. Frisbee flying, girl watching, snoozing in class are perfect examples. If there ever was heaven on earth, it has to be living at a college. I was able to eat, drink, sleep and do almost anything I wanted as much as I wanted whenever and wherever I wanted. It is no wonder that we are called permissive. Naturally, there had to be a balance of studying to continue this blessed utopia. If it wasn't for solving the problems of the world, the college life would be a total frivolous experience. Let's have a cheer for frivolous experiences! I guess we all take ourselves too seriously so it is healthy to enjoy our leisure time. With the improvements in technology, free time has increased dramatically in the past few years. Many unions are pushing for and getting a four day work week. Some people are having difficulty deciding what to do with themselves. Sports and television watching grow to entertain the idle minds. It has to be the simplest mental habit to let the tube think for us. The networks should be commended for their good films and educational shows that give people a common window of the world to see these artistic productions.

The man at leisure often shows his real character. He may be dull at work, he may feel like he is only one chemist or engineer in a company that has 17,000 but watch him at leisure and he can become the Walter Mitty hero he thinks he really is. He grabs his golf clubs and hits one long drive or makes one tough putt and he walks like Jack Nicklaus. He puts away one overhead slam in tennis and he is accepting the Wimbledon trophy like Jimmy Connors. The fisherman and hunter daydream of early pioneers when this activity was a way of survival.

Leisure time planning is often more important than goal planning in a person's career. The time and money spent on vacations is amazing. Travel to climates where we lie in the sun sipping tall, cool drinks are yearly realities. On my honeymoon in Nassau, in the Bahamas, I felt the urge to do everything and see all there was to see instead of what one does on a honeymoon. I had to climb the top of the Queen's stairs; walk in the fortresses, touch the cannons, play blackjack in the casinos, watch the Las Vegas type floorshow, play golf and tennis, and would you believe para-sailing.

For people who do not know what para-sailing is, I must describe this experience. It costs $15 and the ride only takes about 5 minutes. My wife and I rode out to a raft on a speed boat taxi. The raft was the starting and landing point of the ride. You wait your turn trying to convince yourself that you are not crazy to be there. The attendants strap you in a parachute-like harness and sit and wait for the motorboat to take off. They hold your parachute out in the wind as the boat starts. I was on the end of a 300 foot rope. I immediately rose to about 150 feet in the air. The jolt of going up was scary. I held onto the upper ropes even though I was strapped in like a hunk of meat on a chain. I floated in the air with the greatest of ease looking over the island and waterways. The wind rocked me back and forth as the boat started to make a circle back to the raft. I had the sudden fear of what I would do is the line breaks. First, I would pray. I came in for a landing, hoping that I hit the raft and not the water. They brought me in on a control pulley where I made a three-point landing with my rear end making the most contact. It looks harder and more difficult than it is, but I still wonder why I did it or what I was trying to prove to myself or my wife.

I believe in short vacations. They clear out the cobwebs of routine living. These short retreats give you a better perspective to your work or responsibilities. The theme of all work and no play makes Jack a dull boy is often true. The proper balance is the key to sanity and peace of mind. Too much of either can destroy the real substance of life. People ask why men work instead of play. It is easily answered. I think you appreciate your play time the most after you worked your hardest. Leisure tine will shape our lives more in the future, so I for one will enjoy lovemaking, gourmet dining, wine tasting, sleeping in, playing sports with friends, and visits with family to the fullest before returning to my work. I still haven't decided if writing is work or play.

SUNDAY MORNING SENSATIONS

Saturday night sins and Sunday morning salvations
Make a person wonder about this glorious celebration
Life in all its mystery unveils a floating fantasy
Of dreams and schemes and fairy tales that some-
times may come true.

We ask this question "Why,"
and hope that we may learn
The reasons that people die
In the seasons as they turn.

Every thought is a revelation,
Our passive acts, our meditation.
As actions become our special prayer
We reveal to God why we are here.

5.

LOVE OF SELF

Thomas Jefferson made the point that by serving our own aspirations we inspire others to greatness. I truly believe in this pure form of selfishness. I cannot think for my fellow man. I speak poorly for what he believes because I am only putting my beliefs in words he approves. I cannot even sure that I perceive objective events as another might. If you ever were witness to an auto accident, you become aware of how conflicting stories about the facts can easily occur. We all have symbols and connotations for people and things that we see.

I have developed a good self concept so it is easy for me to love myself. I fit in perfectly with my view of the world's harmony. I have my head together regarding my proper respect for God, family and country. I could easily play for Knute Rockney's football team on my healthy attitude alone. If I didn't love myself so much I could not write and tell you about me. I don't care if you find this essay boring or inspiring because it means some thing to me.

Every individual can inspire others in their chosen field. Chemists, engineers, doctors, and secretaries all command respect when they apply their trade in a single goal of satisfying themselves with their efforts. Inventors were trying to make themselves rich by their inventions. Our founding fathers knew the wealth they could possess if they were not controlled by the British. I am not recommending that our motives be always money oriented because we would lose our self respect if this was our only goal. The self awareness that we have when we finish a job well done is pure pleasure. The thrill of victory is fantastic when we climb over the final obstacle on our way to success. We admire the great men of the past, not for the wealth they accumulated, but for their persistent efforts. We model our lives after these leaders because we want similar success. To be the best in your field, you should always study the methods of past heroes. A combination of reproduction and innovation will almost always produce a better result. The technician and engineer of today is improving the machine and formulas of the past because they want something better for themselves. Let the editorial writers claim how altruistic our country is. The realist knows that decisions made on selfish grounds compete the best in the world's eye because all other countries operate on the same basis. The "what's in it for me" philosophy is the most important question to be answered in every situation. As a salesman, I know that unless I can clearly show to my customer how he can benefit economically or project his self image better, I cannot make the sale.

A healthy self-love attitude is perhaps the most important element in a successful venture. People who put themselves down or deny themselves will remain on the bottom of the pile unrewarded and disregarded. This theory of self-love does not condemn sacrifice, brotherhood, team spirit, or other loyalties, they are all necessary in achieving a strong self concept.

When we are trying to better ourselves, joining organizations, forming partnerships and cooperating with the team are often necessary. We gain strength from this collective spirit. But we must never forget that no one in the world knows what is good for me but me. Once we attain the age of reason, we are compelled to use this great gift. Letting other people make decisions that strongly affect our lives is a subtle form of slavery. Be yourself, live for yourself and love yourself and others will love you more for it.

I SAW IT WRITTEN

Danger! Looking at the sun may be harmful to your health
It was there on the side, a law to abide.
From a world that limits the gifts of God
I decided it was time to run and hide.

No longer could I stop, stand or park
Or heaven forbid if I played on the beach
I'd surely be arrested if I walked in the dark.
Actions like these are lacking in class
But there is no such thing as rule the mass.

Just to be able to breathe fresh air
Or be allowed to live here or there
Is a small request from a normal fellow
Who detests the life that makes him hollow.

Yes, I saw it written everywhere
To crush the different and be aware
Of the one who is to come or the one has gone
In this confused, silly world
I wonder why to die is to live and to live is to die.

I saw yet another sign that read
"Thou shalt not kill."
Yet this law was covered by a mist of hatred
That encouraged the extinction of the enemy
And it became right to do wrong
While the song of the prophet was scorned and silenced.

6.

POLITICS AND GOVERNMENT

We have a new president, Jimmy Carter. We see new hopes, dreams, promises from a corrupted system. The plans of our founding fathers were tremendously simple. A check and balance system made every part of the three branches of government responsible to the others. The lawmakers were held in the highest esteem as they defended states rights and minority interests. The president was a leader who set the tone of the country. He was supposed to be a moral man who made decisions based on reason and compassion. His wisdom was preferred over the possibility of mob rule. The writers of our Constitution wrote the greatest document to individual liberty and worth ever recorded. They wanted no king or possible tyrant who could sell privileges and wage foreign wars for fun and profit. The judicial branch of government was revered the most. Sitting on worldly thrones, these wisest of our wise would create a world based on law. Men must live by certain laws for any fair kind of social harmony.

I thought it is important that we remember our ancestors' good intentions. We have made ourselves their bastards. I realize this language sounds strong from a truly patriotic American, but I believe this to be true. Elected representatives were supposed to vote as their constituency felt, yet this majority theme has been overruled by special interest groups. It seems that if you can't afford to have a lobby for your cause, your cause is not worth much. Almost every major corporation and minority group has paid con men in Washington who pay our supposedly honest Congressmen to protect their trade or industry. If the Congressman accepts the payment, he is a whore to the concept of the democratic system. They are not alone. We, the American people, have gradually given our precious American freedom away to this federal octopus. We cannot call our government "Father" because we do not know who he is. That surely makes us bastards.

At one time the government was by, for, and of the people. The people themselves were supposed to rule themselves through delegated, properly elected authorities. This republic form of democracy was working great until the American people let themselves be fooled. Government and big business formed alliances to get rich at the little man's expense. This back scratching by big shots was based on a mutual growth scheme. I'll let you get fat, if you let me. This gluttony begot labor unions to counteract the balance of power. This was the same system of corruption on a blue color level. The union chiefs were golfing on union dues while helping the little man get an occasional night out at the putt-putt course.

The American people since World War I have asked the government which had become almost completely removed from the average man, to lie to him, to make him feel better. We allowed this friend to become a liar and jackal. It pretended to protect us while it told us sweet lies. It said "I guarantee you no depressions, job uncertainties, plenty of food and old age care if you let me do your thinking for you." It only asked us for more and more taxes every year to pay for its schemes at social planning. Happy days used to come without a price tag, but now they mean defense spending contracts and farm supports. The government bureaucrats were supposed to have answers, yet their answer to a problem was usually just more money to solve the problem. They were afraid to tell us the real answer that government cannot legislate morality. It tries to solve problems by increased spending. It can only devalue everything by wasted expenditures. We asked to be lied to and they did a great job. They warned us about the dangers of Communism, they diverted our attention through social programs whose department heads answer to no one. We fail to realize that if they produce the solution they were created to produce, they would no longer be needed. So, to continue their economic and moral existence, they had to fail and tell us silly reasons for their need of more funding.

All this red tape in government can be corrected. It is *not* an incurable monster. There are some idealistic and realistic Congressmen who propose Sunset bills that make every government program and department naturally expire, unless it can truly prove to the governing bodies who represent the overtaxed American that they are absolutely needed. We have allowed Republicans and Democrats to promise us reform, peace and prosperity, but we have never demanded it. I hope that this new "'why" generation will continue to press for honest answers. The vigil of government reform is probably the most important stop to regaining our values. Let's stop blaming government and start correcting it through intelligent elimination. Making peace with Government comes easily. Simplify, simplify, simplify.

GOOD GUYS GET SHOT

Cannons roared while crowds cheered
The armies were extended beyond the shore
The lonely man prayed for unity
While others received their liberty.

And from the armies of the night,
A nation was burnt and doused was the light.
A hope was felt throughout the land
As castles were built upon the sand.

The dreams of the future slowly faded
When a mystery mangled a mountain of a man
The chains of equality dragged along
With the prophet who preached for eternal peace.

His efforts were silenced and then exploited
Yet his truth triumphs and still marches on.
From disgust to dissent flew the eagle
As thousands thought no end was near
To a perverted placement by a stubborn snake.

Yet a spark arose from a courageous rebel
Who defied the foundations of a phony system
His spark was felt but flickered out.
As hatred and heaven took their course.

The oracle proclaims that man must die
And the faceless mass accept this lot
But I can't help but wonder why
It's mostly the good guys who get shot.

7.

PATRIOTISM

I find patriotism to be a much debated topic. The Kennedy legacy left us the thought "Ask not what your country can do for you, but what you can do for your country." I remember reading it on my milk glass before walking to high school at the impressionable age of 14. This quote seemed to have a certain magic. It was plastered everywhere commercially. I did not realize then that a blind devotion to that principle would eventually go against my present libertarian beliefs. The idea of an individual surrendering his will to the state for whatever the state wanted to do with this mindless robot, is repulsive to me now. It certainly was a patriotic idea at the time. Everyone defines patriotism in their own terms. From an allegiance to government that was nurtured in the '30s under F.D.R. we had millions ready to follow government doctrines to their enslaved death. All too quickly patriotism reared an ugly, parochial head.

Lee Harvey Oswald's patriotism to this country was certainly absent in his successful assassination of President

Kennedy. Many people feel that he had conspirators. Were they loyal to Russia, Cuba or whom? Somehow, Sirhan Sirhan's devotion to the Arabian people led him to believe Robert Kennedy must be stopped. Martin Luther King felt patriotic only when black people were treated fairly. Who knows what ideals his assassin felt? L.B.J. in his own mind was trying to be patriotic when he attempted to help South Vietnamese people fight the North Vietnamese and their Communist supporters. The draft dodgers, deserters, conscientious objectors and protesters felt that they must oppose an unjust war out of a sense of patriotism. I was at the largest peace demonstration in the history of the world in November, 1969, and their message was sincere. These people did not want to burn flags and urinate on the Washington monument. They loved their country. They did not want to leave it—they wanted to correct it. Sure, there were radicals who enjoyed chaos, but they were a slim minority.

The war and the draft was ended as Nixon tried to bring us all together again. He candy-coated his activities with the phrase "Peace with Honor." The country was so torn apart that they looked for leadership anywhere, no matter how dishonest it might be. The American people kept asking their government to lie to them, at which it had become very efficient, willing and ready. People were certainly not asking what they could do for their country, but were wondering what their country was doing to them. They ask this question, "why be patriotic to a corrupt government waging an illegal war for questionable reasons?" This put the concept of patriotism in the public spotlight.

The '70s put the public debate of patriotism on a back burner, as conflicting groups attempted to find their own inner peace. The shootings at Kent State University and the casualties of Vietnam suddenly made the practice of open patriotism dangerous.

Just when our wounds started to heal, the Watergate scandal of 1972 was uncovered. For two years, deeper diggings into government corruptions made the average citizen distrustful of almost all politicians. Our liberties and sacred trusts were stolen and concealed. These political crimes were being covered over by government security. Nixon attempted to use the American flag to cover his lies. His own ego and sense of personal historical importance led to his downfall. The White House tapes depicted a low level of morality existing in our executive branch. The Justice Department seemed to be in existence to extend its own isolated interests. How can anyone understand patriotism through this unholy mess? Somehow the worst form of government ever tried with the exception of all others which we call democracy, seemed to pass another test.

The light of democracy shone again through Gerald Ford, the successor of the disgraced, resigning President Nixon. This country has been too busy fighting recession, depression, inflation and various shortages to consider how strong their patriotism is. Too many people are struggling just to make ends meet to wonder if democracy will outlast Communism or if America is now stronger. If you ask a citizen what he can do for his country, he might answer, "Look what it has done to me." I consider myself a patriot because I live within certain geographical boundaries with people whom I share a common history, language and culture. I support free enterprise, the democratic concept of a representative republic and the worth of an individual in the country. I fear our government makes the American look smaller in his own eyes. He feels he is helpless against a system too large to influence. The true patriot will vote the rascals out and support the ones who can represent the individual and the majority without compromising the security or the liberty of each. I realize that this is asking for "a hell of a lot," but patriotism is an ideal worth reaching for and fighting for because without it, we are a defenseless, defeated people.

P.S. President Ford said in his State of the Union message, "To be an American citizen, is still the greatest privilege in the world today." I know he is right.

DRIPS AND DROPS

A drip is a warning while a drop is a bomb
We overlook signals that we should have looked over.
Had we listened to the beautiful we could now be like them
But the drips went unheeded while the drops succeeded.
What a time it was when rain was a blessing from a merciful sky
But mercy has gone and man is here to make sure that the drops will fall.
I have a feeling that the drips I see
Must be stopped by more than poetry.

8.

MONEY AND MATERIAL POSSESSIONS

I have been a salesman for many companies, selling different products. This job is an important one. I once learned that on the average, every salesman keeps 40 people working. If a product is not sold, the manufacturer need not make any more products. Management would have no one to manage and money will not make more money. I have been in the money business regardless of what company I represented. It is the most common single unit that all people in a capitalist society share. The dollar is the largest motivation of all people. If someone in the business world denies this, he is a hypocrite. They say that money is the root of all evil, yet I believe sincerely that the lack of money is the root of all our vices. When a person honestly sells his talents to a company or government service, he bargains honestly with his time. If he works hard and is paid well, the good bargain produces a healthy society. Many people sell themselves short by agreeing too soon.

It is interesting to see the opposite situation occurs when a person gains a high position through favoritism instead of through talent. The overpaid workers drag everyone down because someone must work harder to cover the gap. The lack of money motivates people to dishonest behavior. People steal others' property and destroy lives. They conspire to become richer without earning wealth. People who beg, borrow and try to beat the money system without honestly bargaining in the free market are a threat to all productive people. The bartering system is the oldest and most proven form of exchange in the history of man. Whether it was a rock for a stick or a cow for a sheep, the first exchange when honestly agreed to by both parties was the beginning of the free enterprise system. The law of supply and demand is now and will always be the best formula for fixing values. The emergence of dishonest exchange brought about the need for a referee in the form of government. This necessary evil of a third party overseeing the exchange of monies is a burden that must be limited. This mediator is charging too much for its services, forcing the honest exchangers of value to seek other means of making money. What happens to all this money is the growth of the standard of living. Almost everyone who travels to other continents comes back with the greater appreciation of America because of our high standards. Certainly, we have hunger, poverty, ghettos, illiteracy and crime. Yet these problems usually occur where the inhabitants do not want to join or try to understand the money system. Other countries have rampant diseases, unsanitary conditions and lower opinions of the value of life. I do not want this to sound like a blind, racial, nationalistic generalization. I do wish to make a comparison in standards of living conditions.

Status seeking and greed are natural growths of this capitalistic system. They are cancers of the mind that destroy individuals, families and companies. If these abuses are not checked, the money system looks like a rat race with no winner. After all forms of exchange are compared, the bottom line seems to be that a country who has a lot of producers of worthwhile goods and services prosper and grow stronger. A nation that has a large percentage of people living off the efforts of others collapses in frustration. Socialistic and dictatorial systems fail for the basic reason of not making the individual wanting to better himself. Why would someone work harder if he is always carrying someone on his back. If every person sees he can be better off for his labors, this person would participate in the money system. He will use his human pride, his strength of will and allegiance of heart to make his world happier. After all the religious and philosophical reasons for living are described, the basic fact remains that the individual is on this earth to be happy. We prefer pleasure over pain.

This pseudo-economic essay was not meant to impress the great money minds of the world but was intended to impress the great money minds of the world but to impress the average man that his perspiration and inspiration is noble. His drive for better clothes, cars and houses may seem full of vanity and misguided gods, yet he is a stronger person by his efforts. Mark Twain in his book *The Gilded Age* best represented the American and his money system. He felt that every American desires to improve his financial and social conditions. Sometimes his dreams and schemes fail and he is disappointed. Yet, it is better for a group or country to have dreams and schemes and sometimes succeed than never grow richer or better in your own eyes and not try. Even in the most corrupt of our economic ages, money making more money has made man a happier creature.

SECURITY

Security is a state of mind
It comes and goes with the tide
Contentment is a fleeting find
Enjoy your time on the ride.

When days are smooth and nights are cool
You make your move and live by the rule.
But when times get rough and the light starts to fade,
You have had enough of the problems you've made.

Confusion is king as the storm moves the sea
You can't do a thing without your security
So learn this well, this lesson I teach
Security can be hell, and hell is within reach.

9.

FAMILY AND HOME

An arctic blast is attacking our house as this extra cold winter hits the frightened northeast. Snow, cold, ice, slush and all of winter's torments do not bother me at all. My family is safe within my home. My tiny, condominium townhouse is warm inside. The fireplace crackles but doesn't smell die to the artificial log. My Sauterne is a golden, semi-sweet, California wine. Our window to the world is a Zenith color 23". This peaceful setting is incomplete without telling you that my lovely wife is sitting on the couch snuggling under an Indian blanket avidly reading a baby book. Our lovely baby daughter is sound asleep and all seems right with the world.

The family is the strongest cohesive unit to which an individual can be loyal in good and bad times. The bonds of blood have no match in strength. Certainly there are close and broken families, but the inner allegiance still remains. Even the prodigal son is welcomed home.

There is a story about a convict who was in prison

for life on a rape, grand larceny and first degree murder charge. This caged animal did not deserve life, he had destroyed and terrorized so many good, innocent people that society's noblest deed might be the death penalty. Yet, his loving mother would come every visiting period and sob to the guards. "Johnny is not a bad boy, he's just confused. Is he getting enough to eat? Can I give him a piece of cake?" This scene depicts the strength of the mother-son bond in the family. I also know every father feels protective to his daughter, especially when younger men come calling to charm her. Daddy's little girl better get home safe and secure or else.

It is a shame that families just get together on special occasions, such as weddings, funerals, and sometimes Christmas. All members of the family see this and do nothing about it. Every family gets so busy in their own affairs that visiting someone who cares about you becomes less important. Brothers, sisters and cousins that grow close and remain tight over the years form an unbreakable bond of respect and loyalty. What greater cure for loneliness can there be than a heart to heart talk or long-distance chat to a family voice. Families make a house a home. Their love for each other makes a love nest out of the wood and bricks they inhabit.

It is easy to tell the difference between a house and a home when one enters it. The splendor of the furniture and the richness of the carpet have no correlation to the human element necessary to make a good home. Home has been called the place where the heart is, or wherever you hang your hat. No matter how humble it is, there's no place like home. All these cliches have some truth, but I like this one the best: Home is the place where you can go that no matter where you have been or what you have done, they still have take you in.

The making of a good home directly reflects the love between husband and wife and parent and child. Never forget the importance of the home and the loyalty of the family. You must fight for it, defend it, protect it and work at making it stronger all the time or else you will become a nobody living nowhere, loving no one. Peace of mind is planted in the home and nurtured through the family.

WHY DO THE CHILDREN SCATTER?

Was there a lion's roar or a lightning strike
that chased the radicals from the mike?
Maybe tired ears turned off their tune
While eager eyes approached the moon.

The rally reasons became a bore
as thousands trickled home from Nixon's war.
Where did they go? Back to the classes?
The violent mob became the mumbling masses.

The children scattered so far and wide
Some got hooked on dope while their leaders died
Others hip on Christ confessed their sins,
While ego freaks looked where to begin.

But for many like me, we accept our fate
and choose for the moment to sit and wait
Yes, we are quiet now and out of sight,
Kent State has taught us that it is useless to fight.

A better way is now our goal
To unify the worldly soul,
The why generation is pensive and meek.
Some inner peace is what we now seek.

10.

CONVERSATION

"Turn it off, turn it off in the middle of the sentence!" This desperate plea was explained by Howard Beale, played by Peter Finch in the popular movie, *Network*. He warned how television was destroying your lives. Children spend more time watching it than they do learning in school. Adults let it think for them. It is true that we are almost all somewhat addicted to it. I argue with my wife over its value. Before radio and television brought us all this amusement, people resorted to the most natural form of entertainment that the human mind was capable of—conversation.

The art of conversation is a lost one. The ability to listen and respond in full, sensible sentences seems to have disappeared in our hectic society. We are so used to a digested form of living that we pass our leisure time grabbing snatches of ideas and messages. Think back to the last intelligent conversation you had with someone. How long did it last? What did you learn? Did you thoroughly express a point without being boring or repeating yourself? I ask these questions because what we call conversation is nothing more than chit chat and gossip exchange.

The ability to make appropriate comments is important in keeping friends. When visiting friends and relatives we must be observant to make comments about weight change or furniture arranging. These attentions make the host feel his or her changes are important.

There are many types of conversations that take different moods. A call home to Mom or Dad must be positive in tone. Oh how a mother worries if she senses that something is wrong. Your health and job status must be reaffirmed because most mothers think that you are always hungry and broke without their support. Listening to the family gossip is a necessary function. Who is getting married and who is dying is more important to older people than me, but this must be transmitted.

Conversations with employers are curious. They are often feared but usually confirming. It seems we are afraid to discover how we are doing in our job. The truth that we are afraid might be depressing so we stupidly avoid contact with our bosses. They usually are appreciative of our efforts and have a lukewarm interest in our problems. They seem concerned yet have no plans to remedy our immediate situations. How many times does an employee help his boss with his personal problems or pressing needs?

Conversations with children are interesting and embarrassing. They are so frank in their comments that we learn the truth or the imagined concept very quickly. Children reflect our speech patterns and vocabulary so it is important that we choose our words when we talk to them. It is helpful to speak to a child with full rights and reasoning ability. Talking down to a child just builds a wall between true communication. Those smart remarks and obscene language have their source in us and our peer group.

Talking to retired people can be the most inspiring and best learning experience that we have. Older people are more aware of situations than we give them credit. They often do not speak about problems bothering them. They suffer in silence as we miss great opportunities to learn from their wisdom. America seems to be one of the few cultures that puts old people aside with little respect for their achievement or knowledge. I had a great experience in college while taking a history course about the Great Depression in the '30s. My mother's father was a worker in the shipyards at Philadelphia in the early growth of labor movements. I was amazed with his memory of people, places and dates at his young age of 72. He could tell me in great detail the events of the time and how they affected him. His sharp memory was refreshing to me and helped me get a high mark on my term paper. His knowledge made me respect opinions of others regardless of whether I agree with them or not. Conversations with people who actually know something and can relate it clearly are very stimulating. I cherish the few friends I have that stimulate my mind and give homage to the great art of conversation that we all should try to develop and improve.

WELCOME HOME SOLDIER

No parade was there, nor waving flag
As a humble valiant man brings home his heavy bag.
A kiss and a hug and a tear and a smile
From the few who are grateful it all seems worthwhile.

Johnny had laid down his gun
and now he must think.
He stares empty at the sun,
as his spirits slowly sink.

He wonders why no one seems to care
that he fought for his country
in that war over there,
Too many had died while politicians lied.
Is there a method to our madness that creates such sadness?
We built this great nation with freedom and dedication
Let us all say amen and begin again

11.

ORGANIZED RELIGION

I punched in at 11:03, took my seat and began to dream. As the double-talk commenced in the mock drama, my mind wandered over the hill and down to the sea. I walked alone on the cool morning sand. The day was probably Sunday. It may have been Thursday, but it didn't matter. The sun smiled down searching spirit and I began my dialogue. Lord, I said feel lost in a maze of confused signs. My values are questioned by all around me. My principles are shattered with uncertainty. I want to do what I feel I must. I want to conform, but ways of conformity sicken me. I revolt from tradition and revelation. I respect their meaning and their worth, but I ask for something more relevant to my time. Words are the problem, Father. Meanings scatter and apply wherever you want them. Letters thrown together to form a sound pleasing to the eager, malignant audience of lust. If words could only mean one thing, or indicate one action, goals could be reached. But how can progress be achieved by those authorities of verbal abuse that through their warping or language they straddle the fence so long that their thighs ache with splinters. How can war mean peace? How can leaving well enough alone improve something? How can moving out of the city improve it? Silence is the cause of growing volcanoes or injustice. When dissent is stifled, the right marches on. The might has the right with no red light in sight. An alterable law laughs at the young and different and attempts to saddle them at every turn. This uncompromising consensus claims to have you on their side, God. How can I dare to fight force with so great a general as yourself? Should I conspire with Satan to improve my life? Lucifer works without discrimination. The Prince of Devils certainly is more honest than the human demigods of gobbledy gook that claim to preserve the race. Lord, I ask Your help to make me a better person every day and beseech Thee for moral strength to search for the truth regardless of the odds of me finding it. The answers to my questions are found in my soul. The task of my life must be to find this inner essence and manifest it for the rest of mankind. Actions must overcome wasteful words. For surely actions tell me that my prayers are heard. The sound of the sea rushing on the shore is beautiful. The revolving of the earth to permit all to enjoy inspiration is magnificent. I am convinced of God's presence when I smell a flower or feel the vibrations of an affectionate group. Changing colors, changing seasons and changing beauty glow in God's eternal state. What a felony it is that the most exulted of God's creatures gives the least glory and praise to the Creator. If these pitiful Aborigines would follow the principles of life that You, Lord, came to exhibit, the masters of this planet would surely be happy and just masters. But instead of observance to the way of the Lord these truants to divine planning had decided to take care of themselves. Such endless concern for physical comfort and security simply leads to more discomfort and insecurity. Devotion to personal gain has split the bridge of heavenly aid. This lack of concern for neighbor has led to a detached state of dereliction. The isolation of individual in a mass state condemns him to loneliness. There is a growing fear that to become involved is to cause trouble. A pragmatic, growing, glorious nation has succumbed to detached Americanism. What a shame it is that such a beautiful country be inhabited by such a wretched people. That sense of community spirit and working together which created the wealth and admiration of the world has expired. God, you have been replaced in this region. Your dominion has ended. A coup d'etat of your perfect rule has been accomplished by a faction of exploiters whose strength seems unlimited. The American god is the dollar bill, a worthless piece of green paper whose power is unmatched on the face of the earth. I wonder why the hypocrites don't put your image on the seal instead of the President's. Honesty should change the inscription "In God We Trust" to "In Money We Have Put All Our Faith." This faith in the worth of a dollar has made the pious cringe with fear. Their institution has been conquered by the dollar. All the world bows and prays to the benefits man has received through the proper investments. Man spends one third of his life working to earn money. Another third is used to spend this earthly entity and the last third of the man's time is consumed in his sleeping hours, dreaming of new ways and means to get more of America's god. Give me strength, oh Lord, to fight my fight against the faithless people and from the impious and deceitful people rescue me, Oh Lord, I pray for an end to this evil.

The bell rings and my daydream ends. Here come the agents of the establishment. Blessed are the money grabbers, for they shall rule the world, by paying the poor to serve them. There is humble Mrs. Nosey observing the latest in fashion her bridge club members are wearing today. That beautiful bonnet must have cost a lot of god. Such serious faces must be masks put on this morning for surely last night they were laughing, drunken, lustful expressions on those false exteriors. The baby's crying sounds more beautiful than the Latin hosannas or the monotone Amens offered by the sometimes attentive audience. There is Mr. Albertson sound asleep as usual. I wish I had the guts enough to snore as loud through another one of the good preacher's sermons. All these young children are pushed into pews by smiling adults who were probably pushed into pews by their parents before them. Such intense brainwashing must be commended. The growth of this institution in the future is secure.

I wonder how much those stained glass windows cost. I am sure the supply of wine in the rectory could feed a couple of thousands dying of thirst. The robes of the well dressed priests could clothe two naked African countries for years. I'll bet if every church were sold; there would be enough money to feed India for a decade. But giving something for nothing is not the American way. All men are equal, but killing the enemy is okay because they are less equal. White and black should live together in peace as long as the whites have their country home and the clean suburbs and the colored struggle in the filthy ghettos. Such contradictions force me to question the reason I am present. I shall not donate one-tenth of my god to this establishment. I shall not force my children to accept this propaganda and indoctrination that this institution promotes. I can certainly praise my God and follow the way of Christ through my actions without having a huge expensive building to utter mumbo-jumbo on a certain day at a certain time. I wonder how many others are standing here now thinking things like I am. Perhaps I could start my own church. I could call it Freelance Christianity. The world could look at me as a pious man, a good American who encourages the good, and if money is earned by promoting the good, it is even better. Or perhaps I could live a simple life and do what I think is right in my conscience to please God and help my fellow man. But that wouldn't be very American, would it? After all, how much God can a person have if he leads a simple life. Punched out at 11:52 and I returned home as holy as I had come.

HUSTLING

Run, talk, hustle.
Make your minutes count.
Every hour add a dollar
To that sacred amount.

It doesn't matter where you find it
Just as long as you can mine it.
Drain as much as you can,
Then start over again.

Hustling on the street,
Trying out my luck.
Convincing the people I meet
To invest another buck.

Support the money machine
An answer to every prayer, the
Hustling American dream
Is for those who are willing to dare.

12

LIBERTY AND INDIVIDUAL CREATIVITY

Our least used liberty is often our own individual creativity. We an are glad to be free people where the government serves at our pleasure. Yet, we do not explore the full sense of the meaning of our liberty. To be just free is not doing enough for ourselves. We have a greater duty to freedom. Our liberty was hard won and should be expanded, not just defended. I love that old song, "Freedom doesn't come like a bird on the wing. Freedom doesn't fall like summer rain. Freedom, freedom is a hard won thing and every generation has got to win it all again. Pass it on to your children, pass it on. You've got to work for it, die for it, live day and night for it and every generation has got to win it all again."

Struggling nations that are very poor and illiterate, yet demanding, do not understand the most important principle of free countries. The individual is the single most important human element in the progress of civilization. Unless the individual is free, respected and encouraged to better himself the whole system is superficial. The dignity and importance of the individual is paramount. The fact that he is not physically owned by a master is not winning the battle. He must be able to choose what he will do with his life in harmony with the rest of God's creatures. Ironically, this decision is not made by the majority of individuals in the world. The decision is made for him by the family, tribe, corporation or state government. He is told to obey and follow orders instead of learning and leading.

Technology has freed Western man. He can work less and produce more with the help of machines. The natural resources of a country do not usually destine it to riches or poverty because technology brings the product and market together. The most noble human resource of all is man's individual creativity. What man does with his freedom determines his self worth. To enjoy the blessings of a liberated people, the citizens should build, create and plan better ways for people to live happily. Americans are accused of being too concerned with material possessions acquiring things. Yes, the warnings of America's great poets in the Romantic age of Emerson and Thoreau are sometimes true. "Things are in the saddle and they ride mankind." It is easy to become a slave to things, whether it is a car, house, job or some worldly goal. All of these alleged evils are part of the individual's effort to reach to the stars and to grab heaven and put it before him. We often paint our utopias with the comfortable surroundings of life. Is it wrong to want to breathe clean air, drink the purest water, be warm in winter, cool in summer and eat the best food? I do not think so. These are extensions of our ego.

We put our stamp of order and control over our lives. These elements of security make us feel happy. They are products of our creativity fighting chaos, poverty and tyranny. When the individual is free to indulge his hard earned dollars in purchasing power, he creates a circle of wealth. We all know that if everyone stopped spending, a depression immediately occurs. The trust in our ability to better ourselves and faith in the consumer system are the essential ingredients to man's future individual creativity. For true peace of mind be proud of our heritage and freedom, and welcome the future of individual creativity. So write that book, paint that picture, secure that patent, try that new business, and for God's sake and your own, be good to yourself. You deserve it.

OH GUIDING LIGHT OF LIBERTY

Oh guiding light of liberty
We ask your help today
To lighten up these dreary years
And lead us on our way.

Oh bell of freedom, sound your chimes
Let all hear freedom's ring.
Save us from these trying times
And lessen hatred's sting.

Oh dove of peace we beg of you
To fly us to your nest,
Renew our faith in this great land
And put our hearts at rest.

Oh guiding light of liberty,
Our need is at its peak.
We pray your light will strengthen us,
And show the peace we seek.

13

THE FUTURE

The future is not as mysterious as you may think. We often say that no one knows the future, and who knows what the future may hold. I think that as a true member of the why generation, I know the future. I do not mean to act like a gypsy fortune teller or prognosticator. I simply mean, I have a good idea of where I am going. It may sound selfish to say that the only interest I have in the future is "what's in it for me," but this is my major concern. Of course, I care about my loved ones, family, friends, country and civilization as a whole, but I can only speak for myself. I can only guess and assume the future for others. I say that I think I know my future because I create it every day. I sow seeds of future events as I am writing this sentence. I believe in the chain of human events in a person's life. I feel we as human beings are a part of the universal whole. There is an inner oneness to our species, if we looked inside of ourselves to that common denominator. Our spirit, heart, guts, soul or whatever you may call it, is growing whether we like it or not. This growth occurs every day in our actions, thoughts and dreams. I make myself today what I will be in the future. All of these things may be happening in some Vonnegut-like space time warp. Qualities of my character that I try to improve on will make me a better person fifteen years from now. Also, the bad habits that I have let increase and multiply will be bigger problems in the future.

At this moment in my life, I am simply a sum total of all my thoughts, words and deeds, implanted on a physical skeleton of bones, chemicals and blood. My appearance is partly my development on my parents' creation. We all go back to the individual and initial spark of the creation of God. This evolving process is somewhat controllable if we are tuned into it. The only meaning to life is that what we put to it. If a person finds life meaningless, he will certainly be a meaningless person with few or more meaningless actions. When a person dies his physical remains are buried or burned and returned to the mother earth. This ash to ash concept of existence is not depressing when you look at the full scope of humanity. I can share in greatest thoughts and inventions of the greatest people who walked the earth. Their spirit and influence will never die. I can walk around the library and read the ideas of the greatest engineers, artists, writers and philosophers of mankind. This immortality is not equally shared. The man who made the desk and the chair I sit at may be dead, but his efforts are still used and appreciated in a smaller utilitarian way. So when I say I know the future, I am only extending the human chain of events to their logical extension.

In the near future, I will write a novel. I will respect my parents more as I grow older. I will become a father and love my children. I will argue with my wife and love her more every day. I will pay taxes. I will become too old to play sports. I will promote libertarian ideals. I will attempt to love my God, myself, and my fellow man with greater intelligence. I know I personally will achieve these actions because everyday I step a little closer to these goals. The people, locations and social events will change but the basic strength of my beliefs and aspirations will become my present attitudes in the future. But what future is there for the why generation? The patient, persistent followers and leaders must have schemes and dreams to accomplish in the days ahead. Here is where my certainty ends and my hopes and fears command my predictions. Whether all these things shall pass is not of my doing but of a grander scheme, which too many people and events can affect.

1. I believe that the why generation will continue to ask the question why, until the answers get better.
2. They will look inward to themselves for greater imagination, dedication and ambition, while most blind people will flock to collective security.
3. They will love themselves in the pure form by developing their abilities to their human peak.

4. The will understand the games that people play and try to be above the enemy without surrendering to their tactics and limited perspectives.
5. They will respect their physical limitations, knowing that the flesh is weak, but it is the only body that we have so we might as well take care of it with good nutrition and sleep.
6. The why generation will be active in politics, where it serves to remove scoundrels and diminish the dominant influence of the state over the individual mind.
7. They will practice the work ethic even when it seems that promotions come to relatives and not those of merit. When all is said and done perspiration and inspiration will prevail.
8. They will love this great country and all its believable and realistic ideals and they will defend it, but not oppress others with it, and lead by example instead of force.
9. They will respect every man's image of his god and his attempts to find him in his heart. This great pursuit must always be free.
10. They will enjoy the fruits of life with their families in their homes. Their leisure time will be full of happiness.
11. They will enjoy the natural comforts and important intangibles of conversation, loyalty and faith with equal relish. A house may consist of bricks

and wood, but a heart and a lot of love are necessary to make a home.

12. The why generation will broadcast the message of freedom and the dignity of the individual until all are free and proud.

13. The why generation will not look to the future for the realization of its goals because the future is now. We make our lives and our world what they are and what they will be from this day to the next. So let us start now and continue forever and always be the why generation.